A POCKET GUIDE TO SACRAMENTAL RECONCILIATION

KEVIN AND MARY O'NEILL
BUILDING BLOCKS OF FAITH SERIES

SOPHIA INSTITUTE PRESS
Manchester, New Hampshire

This revised and expanded 2022 edition of the Building Blocks of Faith series *A Pocket Guide to Sacramental Reconcilliation* is based on the 2021 Storytel Press publication of the same title. Text and images have been adapted from the Building Blocks of Faith series' *Catechism of the Seven Sacraments*.

Copyright © 2021, 2022 by Kevin and Mary O'Neill

Cover by Perceptions Studios

Printed in the United States of America. All rights reserved.

Scripture texts in this work are taken from the New American Bible, revised edition © 2010, 1991, 1986, 1970 Confraternity of Christian Doctrine, Washington, D.C. and are used by permission of the copyright owner. All Rights Reserved. No part of the New American Bible may be reproduced in any form without permission in writing from the copyright owner.

Excerpts from the English translation of the Catechism of the Catholic Church for use in the United States of America copyright © 1994, United States Catholic Conference, Inc.—Libreria Editrice Vaticana. English translation of the Catechism of the Catholic Church: Modifications from the Editio Typica copyright © 1997, United States Conference of Catholic Bishops—Libreria Editrice Vaticana.

LEGO®, the brick configuration, and the minifigure are all trademarks of the LEGO Group, which does not sponsor, authorize, or endorse this book.

No part of this book may be reproduced, stored in a retrieval system, or transmitted in any form, or by any means, electronic, mechanical, photocopying, or otherwise, without the prior written permission of the publisher, except by a reviewer, who may quote brief passages in a review.

Sophia Institute Press
Box 5284, Manchester, NH 03108
1-800-888-9344
www.SophiaInstitute.com

Sophia Institute Press® is a registered trademark of Sophia Institute.

print ISBN: 978-1-64413-876-2
ebook ISBN: 978-1-64413-877-9

Library of Congress Control Number: 2022948593

> FULTON, CAN YOU REMIND ME WHAT I SHOULD DO WHEN I GO TO THE SACRAMENT OF RECONCILIATION?

> SURE, CYNTHIA!

> FIRST YOU ASK THE HOLY SPIRIT IN PRAYER TO HELP YOU REMEMBER YOUR SINS.

> THEN YOU DO AN EXAMINATION OF CONSCIENCE BY CALLING TO MIND YOUR PAST THOUGHTS, WORDS, ACTIONS, AND NEGLECTS. YOU CAN USE THE TEN COMMANDMENTS AS YOUR GUIDE.

CCC 1453, CCC 1454

PRAYER BEFORE RECONCILIATION

Oh loving, merciful, and triune God, do assist me to fully examine my conscience and grant me true sorrow for my sins. Strengthen me through Thy divine assistance to detest my sins, humbly confess them, and avoid sin throughout my life. I ask through the intercession of Mary, refuge of sinners, all the holy angels, especially my guardian angel, and all of the saints of God, that I may recall how I have strayed from God's divine will for my life, which is to know, love, and serve Him through my thoughts, words, and deeds. Amen.

STEPS TO A SACRAMENTAL RECONCILIATION

1. Begin with a prayer to ask the Holy Spirit to help you recall your sins and examine your conscience (recall your sins, number and kind).

2. Go into the confessional and kneel (or sit). The priest will say, "In the name of the Father, and of the Son, and of the Holy Spirit." Make the sign of the cross and say, "**Amen.**"

3. Then say, "**Bless me, Father, for I have sinned. It has been ___ (amount of time) since my last confession.**"

4. Say, "**I am sorry for** ___ (list your sins beginning with all mortal sins and then proceeding to venial sin). Then say, "**For these and all of my sins, I am truly sorry.**"

5. The priest may give some words of guidance, and then he will give you a penance (prayer to say or kind act to do).

6. The priest will say, "Now make your Act of Contrition." You say, "**O my God, I am heartily sorry for having offended Thee, and I detest all my sins, because I dread the loss of Heaven and the pains of hell, but most of all because they offend Thee, my God, Who art all good and deserving of all my love. I firmly resolve, with the help of Thy grace, to confess my sins, to do penance, and to amend my life. Amen.**"

7. You receive absolution (forgiveness), when the priest says, "**Through the ministry of the Church, may God give you pardon and peace, and I absolve you of your sins, in the name of the Father, and of the Son, and of the Holy Spirit.**" Make the sign of the cross and say, "**Amen.**"

8. The priest says, "Go in peace." You respond, "**Thanks be to God.**" Leave the confessional and do your penance as immediately as possible, thanking God for His love, mercy, and forgiveness.

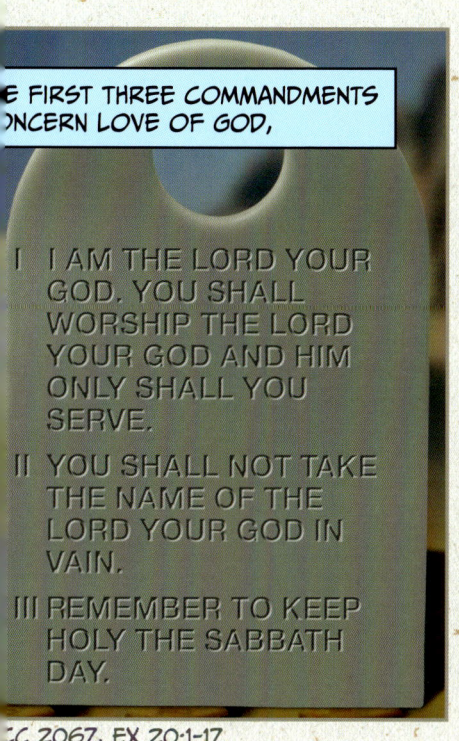

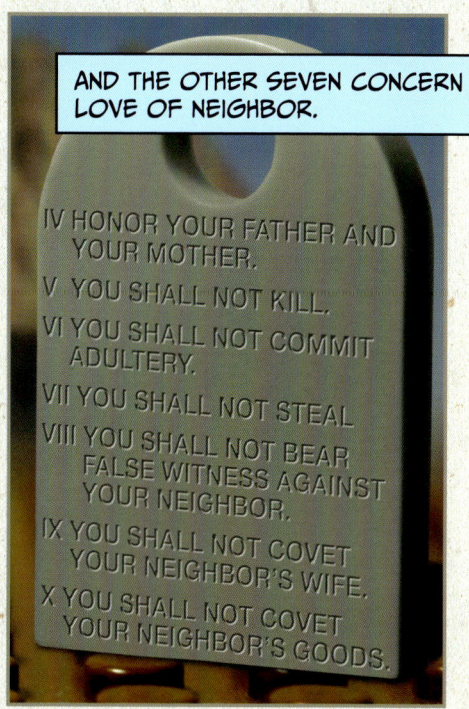

THE FIRST THREE COMMANDMENTS CONCERN LOVE OF GOD,

AND THE OTHER SEVEN CONCERN LOVE OF NEIGHBOR.

I. I AM THE LORD YOUR GOD. YOU SHALL WORSHIP THE LORD YOUR GOD AND HIM ONLY SHALL YOU SERVE.

II. YOU SHALL NOT TAKE THE NAME OF THE LORD YOUR GOD IN VAIN.

III. REMEMBER TO KEEP HOLY THE SABBATH DAY.

IV. HONOR YOUR FATHER AND YOUR MOTHER.

V. YOU SHALL NOT KILL.

VI. YOU SHALL NOT COMMIT ADULTERY.

VII. YOU SHALL NOT STEAL.

VIII. YOU SHALL NOT BEAR FALSE WITNESS AGAINST YOUR NEIGHBOR.

IX. YOU SHALL NOT COVET YOUR NEIGHBOR'S WIFE.

X. YOU SHALL NOT COVET YOUR NEIGHBOR'S GOODS.

CCC 2067, EX 20:1-17

EXAMINATION OF CONSCIENCE

I am the Lord your God. You shall not have strange gods before me. Do I put other things before God (e.g., TV, games, money, etc.)? Do I pray every day? Do I thank God for all He has done for me? Do I use my time and talents to know, love, and serve God and help others to do the same? Have I been curious about or participated in anything that the Church knows is associated with the devil and evil spirits such as a seance or ouija board?

You shall not take the name of the Lord your God in vain. Have I used God's name in vain by calling upon Him to condemn someone or something? Have I used God's name as an expression of surprise or while not praying? Have I sworn or made a promise in God's name that I did not keep?

Remember to keep holy the Lord's Day. Have I faithfully attended Mass on Sundays and Holy Days of Obligation? Did I allow myself to be distracted or talk during Mass? Did I listen carefully to God's Word at Mass and take time to reflect on it and implement it?

4. **Honor your father and mother.** Have I talked back to or disrespected my parents, grandparents, teachers, or others in authority? Have I fully obeyed my parents and so forth? Do I willingly complete my chores, duties, and responsibilities?

5. **You shall not kill.** Have I injured my own body? Was I angry toward others or have I hated someone? Do I fight with others? Have I told others to do inappropriate things? Have I cursed, gossiped, or talked badly about others? Have I refused to forgive someone?

6. **You shall not commit adultery.** Did I treat my body and others' bodies with the respect and dignity given to them by God? Have I remained chaste in thought and deed for my state in life? Have I been modest in thought, word, and deed? Did I read magazines, watch movies, or look at pictures that are inappropriate? Have I told or listened to inappropriate stories or jokes?

7. **You shall not steal.** Have I desired to steal anything? Have I stolen money or other things? Have I returned anything that I have stolen? Have I destroyed something that belonged to another? Have I returned things that I have borrowed? Did I cheat on my schoolwork? Have I done what is required of me in my schoolwork, my chores at home, or any work for which I am being paid?

8. **You shall not bear false witness against your neighbor.** Have I lied? Have I gossiped? Have I told the whole truth, without omission? Do I make up stories about others? Have I spread the faults of others unnecessarily?

9. **You shall not covet your neighbor's wife.** Have I kept chaste thoughts? Have I prayed for and taken time to discern God's will for my vocation in life? Have I prayed for and encouraged holy marriages?

10. **You shall not covet your neighbor's goods.** Have I desired to steal money or things from others? Was I jealous of others? Have I wanted to destroy what others have so they could not have it?

THE SEVEN CAPITAL SINS:

Pride, avarice (greed), lust, wrath (extreme anger), gluttony, envy, and sloth.

THE TWO GREAT COMMANDMENTS OF LOVE:

1. You shall love the Lord your God with all your heart, and with all your soul, and with all your mind, and with all your strength.
2. You shall love your neighbor as yourself.

AFTER YOU HAVE EXAMINED YOUR CONSCIENCE AND KNOW THE SINS YOU NEED TO CONFESS, GO TO THE CONFESSIONAL AND KNEEL OR SIT.

YOU BEGIN BY MAKING THE SIGN OF THE CROSS AS THE PRIEST SAYS,

IN THE NAME OF THE FATHER, AND OF THE SON, AND OF THE HOLY SPIRIT. AMEN.

THEN YOU SAY,

BLESS ME FATHER FOR I HAVE SINNED. IT HAS BEEN (HOW LONG) SINCE MY LAST CONFESSION.

THEN TELL HIM YOUR SINS AND HOW MANY TIMES YOU COMMITTED EACH ONE. COMPLETE YOUR LIST BY SAYING,

FOR THESE AND ALL MY PAST SINS, I AM TRULY SORRY.

THE PRIEST MAY THEN TALK TO YOU TO GIVE YOU GUIDANCE ON HOW TO AVOID THESE SINS IN THE FUTURE.

HE WILL GIVE YOU A PENANCE, WHICH IS A WAY FOR YOU TO MAKE AMENDS FOR YOUR SINS. IT'S USUALLY A TASK SUCH AS A FEW PRAYERS TO RECITE OR AN ACT OF KINDNESS TOWARD OTHERS.

CCC 1480   CCC 1494

HE WILL ASK YOU TO RECITE AN ACT OF CONTRITION LIKE THIS ONE:

Act of Contrition

O my God, I am heartily sorry for having offended Thee, and I detest all my sins, because I dread the loss of Heaven, and the pains of hell; but most of all because they offend Thee, my God, Who are all good and deserving of all my love. I firmly resolve, with the help of Thy grace, to confess my sins, to do penance, and to amend my life. Amen.

CCC 1459-146

FINALLY, YOU WILL BE ABSOLVED (SET FREE) OF YOUR SINS.

THROUGH THE MINISTRY OF THE CHURCH, MAY GOD GIVE YOU PARDON AND PEACE, AND I ABSOLVE YOU FROM YOUR SINS, IN THE NAME OF THE FATHER, AND OF THE SON, AND OF THE HOLY SPIRIT.

AMEN.

CCC 1449

THE PRIEST WILL SAY,

AND YOU RESPOND,

GO IN PEACE.

THANKS BE TO GOD.

WHEN YOU LEAVE THE CONFESSIONAL, YOU SHOULD KNEEL IN A PEW, THANK GOD FOR FORGIVING YOUR SINS, AND COMPLETE YOUR PENANCE AS SOON AS POSSIBLE.

DO YOU HAVE MORE QUESTIONS ABOUT RECONCILIATION? HERE ARE SOME COMMON QUESTIONS WITH HELPFUL SHORT ANSWERS AND RESOURCES:

WHAT DOES RECONCILIATION DO?

When you confess your mortal sins in the Sacrament of Reconciliation, they are forgiven and Sanctifying grace is restored, you are reunited with God and His Church, and the eternal punishment is removed. When you regularly confess your venial sins, these are forgiven and you are spiritually strengthened against the possibility of committing mortal sin (CCC 1440, 1468-1469, 1473).

WHAT IS A MORTAL SIN?

There are three conditions for a sin to be mortal: 1. Grave (serious) matter: intrinsically evil and immoral. 2. Full knowledge: know that it is wrong. 3. Deliberate consent: you freely choose to do it (CCC 1857).

HOW OFTEN SHOULD I GO TO CONFESSION?

The second precept of the Catholic Church requires you to make a sacramental confession at least once per year when you are aware of having committed grave sin (mortal sin). It is necessary that this be done before you can fulfill the third precept of the Church: "You shall receive the sacrament of the Eucharist at least once during the Easter season." You should make a sacramental confession as immediately as possible if you are in the state of mortal sin and you should refrain from receiving Holy Communion because it is an additional mortal sin to receive the Eucharist in the state of mortal sin. Venial sin can be taken away in some special ways, such as by the sprinkling of holy water (the Asperges) during the Penitential Rite of the Mass and the reception of the Holy Eucharist when you are consciously sorry for your venial sins. However, it is a good practice to confess your venial sins sacramentally at least once per year and even to do so regularly during the year, such that many priests recommend confession monthly (CCC 1456-1458, 1493).

DO I NEED TO CONFESS ALL OF MY SINS?

Yes, a confession is only valid if you confess all of your recalled mortal sins. This is why a thorough examination of conscience is prudent before receiving this sacrament (CCC 1456). The Church also strongly recommends that we confess our venial sins to help us fight against evil tendencies (CCC 1458).

WHICH SACRAMENTS FORGIVE SINS?

Baptism, Reconciliation, Communion (venial only), and Extreme Unction all forgive sin.

WHAT ARE THE SEVEN CAPITAL (DEADLY) SINS?

The Seven Capital Sins are pride, avarice, envy, wrath, lust, gluttony, and sloth. We should work to replace these sins by practicing the Seven Capital Virtues, which are humility, liberality, chastity, meekness, temperance, kindness, and diligence. Through continuous effort and with the help of God's grace, virtues can increase and vices can diminish, but we must also avoid the near occasion of sin (CCC 1866).

WHERE IS CONFESSION IN THE BIBLE?

In John 20:21-23, Jesus gave the apostles the authority to forgive sins. This divine power and authority has been faithfully passed on in the Catholic Church in the Catholic priesthood through the centuries and will be so until the end of time.

WHY DO I NEED TO CONFESS MY SINS TO A PRIEST, SINCE GOD ALONE HAS THE AUTHORITY TO FORGIVE SINS?

Jesus, who is God, extended this authority to His apostles to carry on His mission in John 20:22. How would the disciples know which sins to forgive or retain, unless they are told to them? Also, in 2 Corinthians 5:16-21, this reconciliation is only available by the power of God and through the ministry of the Church instituted by Christ Himself. In Matthew 16:19, Peter was given the keys of the Kingdom, to bind and loose sin. This authority was over Heaven and earth (CCC 1441-1442).

EXPLORE THE ENTIRE
BUILDING BLOCKS OF FAITH SERIES

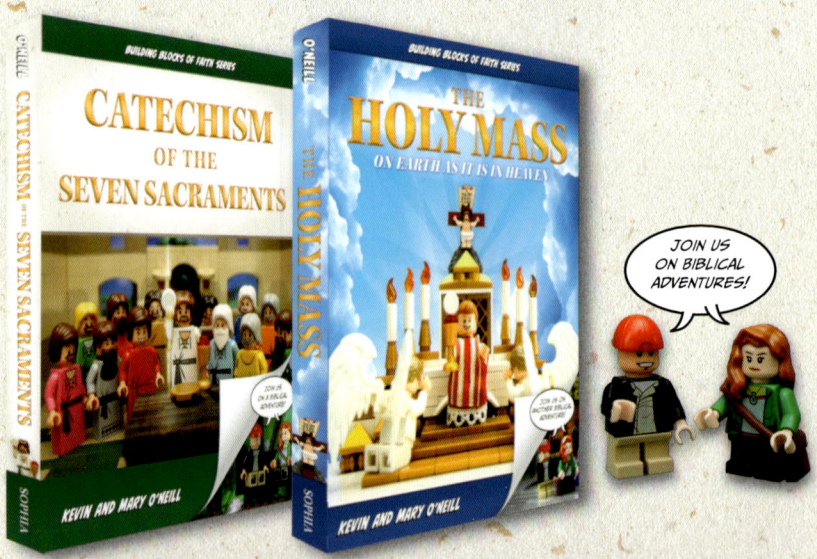

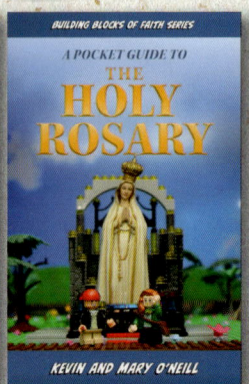

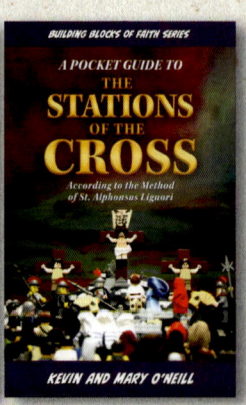

JOIN US ON BIBLICAL ADVENTURES!

The ***Building Blocks of Faith*** series works to create and share solidly orthodox materials to help families build their own domestic churches, and, in turn, to build and strengthen the Body of Christ. Our books use typology to explain the foundations of the Faith. We illustrate our graphic novels by building, designing, and photographing intricate sets — built with your child's favorite building-block toys! We strive to spread the Gospel, help the Faith come alive, create disciples, and promote the call to evangelization, as we do our part to build God's Kingdom.

www.sophiainstitute.com/BuildingBlocks